oy!

Derek.

GAMBA
SIMPLE SEAFOOD
COOKING

SPECIAL
ROAST WHOLE SEABASS
WITH ROAST PEPPERS,
PRAWNS + THAI SAUCE
£17·95

FISHMONGER

GAMBA

SIMPLE SEAFOOD

COOKING

DEREK MARSHALL

INTRODUCED BY BRYAN BURNETT

First published 2000

New edition published 2003

by Black & White Publishing Ltd

ISBN 1902927 91 5

Copyright © Ambermount Ltd 2003

Introduction copyright © Bryan Burnett 2000

British Library Cataloguing in Publication Data:
A catalogue record for this book is available
from the British Library.

Photography by Alan Donaldson

Wine information supplied by Jane Meek

Printed and bound by Bookprint S.L.

CONTENTS

Foreword

The first edition of *Gamba, Simple Seafood Cooking* has sold in excess of 4000 copies. The success of the book and the positive feedback that has been received, has prompted this new edition and an opportunity to add even more of Derek's favourite recipes.

The Gamba cook book is a testament to the outstanding cooking skills of Derek and his talent in 'keeping it simple' and it gives me great pleasure to see his dishes displayed in such glorious colour.

Gamba has been open since October 1998 and apart from a three-week period of enforced closure in February 1999 (due to a mindless late-night intruder and arsonist), has managed to establish itself as a popular destination for Glaswegians as well as visitors from around Scotland and the globe!

Since the last edition was published, the restaurant has continued to win coveted titles; including Best Restaurant in the Auchentoshan "Spirit of Glasgow" Awards for two consecutive years.

I thank every member of our team at Gamba: Derek's brigade in the kitchen, Gregor Munn's excellent front of house staff and those unsung heroes behind the scenes, without whose efforts this book would not be before you today.

Finally, a successful restaurant would not be busy without the key ingredients . . . the customers! To all of you a very big thanks.

Alan Tomkins
(The partner who doesn't do the cooking!)

GAMBA

Gamba Seafood Restaurant
225a West George Street,
Glasgow, Scotland,
G2 2ND

Telephone 00 44 (0) 141 572 0899
e-mail info@gamba.co.uk
www.gamba.co.uk

YOU MIGHT FIND IT DIFFICULT TO COMPREHEND BUT THERE ARE PEOPLE OUT THERE WHO DON'T LIKE FISH.

You might find it difficult to comprehend but there are people out there who don't like fish.

I mean, who doesn't get excited at the thought of a big bowl of chunky fish soup, an appetizing plate of garlicky grilled sardines or a bit of plaice with lemon and parsley butter? What could be more splendid than sitting down to a risotto of lobster and baby asparagus or getting tucked in to a comforting fishcake with a big bowl of salty and crisp fat chips?

Fish can be all things to all people – a quick after work tea of a bit of grilled salmon, a dinner party dish of whole sea bass stuffed with fragrant herbs and spices or a warming winter breakfast of smoked haddock and poached egg.

For a country that produces so much fine seafood, until recently Scotland has had remarkably few really good fish restaurants. Head chef at Gamba, Derek Marshall, wanted to change that.

"We had a situation in Glasgow where you could eat good food from every continent in the world but it was nearly impossible to find simple but imaginative Scottish seafood at a reasonable price.

"I had wanted to open a fish restaurant for years, because for most chefs the fish station is the most challenging and exciting part of any kitchen. At this time, working as Head Chef at Papingo Restaurant in Glasgow, I discovered that there existed a similar keen interest in creating just such an establishment, which culminated in a partnership with my then employers.

"Fish can be over done a lot of the time," maintains Derek Marshall. "You don't want to put too many ingredients into it or else you'll take some of the flavour away from the fish. The joy of fish is that it's so easy and simple to cook.

"Actually one of the other reasons for keeping it simple was the size of the kitchen in the premises we had found. Imagine something the size of six telephone boxes and you're on the right track.

"We were after a traditional Victorian Glasgow location. The place we found in West George Street was a former merchant's townhouse. The idea of it being in a basement was appealing as it wasn't until you got down the stairs and entered the restaurant that you had any idea what it was going to be like."

With recent trips to Portugal influencing the Mediterranean interior colours and atmosphere, a strong "Iberian" influence is present in the style of Gamba.

An impetuous notion to order tiled murals from a local tile maker near Loule, in the Algarve, on the strength of a sketch on a scrap of paper and an anglo-Portuguese conversation, fortuitously proved to be a success – but were unpacked on their arrival amidst much trepidation!

"WE DIDN'T WANT THE DÉCOR TO BE TOO OBTRUSIVE. WE WERE AFTER AN ATTRACTIVE, RESTFUL VENUE WHERE THE MAIN EVENT IS THE FOOD. SIMPLE!"

Although the food in Gamba is simple in it's execution no-one could ever describe it as dull. On a typical menu you might find dishes like fillets of bream with asparagus, mussels and a scallop cream...so good it makes you stop mid-conversation. It's the kind of food that makes you want to keep it all to yourself. Only after much pleading would you agree to share with best friends and lovers.

Although the name comes from the Mediterranean, (Portuguese for prawn), the inspiration for the food at Gamba came from around the globe. Sashimi with pickled ginger sits alongside Thai fishcakes with Swiss chard and sweet Thai jelly. Closer to home wild Tay salmon with redcurrant and rosemary is on the same menu as Arbroath smoked haddock and black pudding mash.

Derek has been cooking for 17 years and started his career at The Fountain restaurant in Glasgow in the early 80s. At the time, The Fountain was one of the finest establishments in the city and for any young chef it was the perfect place to get a grounding in classical French cookery. This was in the days before "fusion food" when dishes like "Sole Meuniere" and "Scampi Provencale" were the height of fashion.

"I realised from the first day I was in the kitchen that this was what I wanted to do with my life. It was extremely hard work – but then again cheffing is hard work. It's not easy but in a busy restaurant kitchen you have to put in the effort if you're going to make it work."

He then spent five years in Jersey including two years at the Grand Hotel, studying the classical tradition and learning to cook with the wonderful seafood found in the waters around Jersey.

When Derek returned to Scotland he found himself at Rogano, which at that time had an unrivalled reputation for it's seafood and was often referred to as the best restaurant in the city. Under the tutelage of head chef, Jim Kerr, Derek learned important lessons for any chef; organisation, consistency and the art of keeping it simple.

"Jim was a big influence on my cooking and is still one of my best mates. He's a great person to hit ideas off and he's always passing on favourite dishes to me. The Scallops and Monkfish en Papillotte on page 89 is one of his."

It has been said many times over the years that a good restaurant is like a great theatre. After all, the aim at the end of the night is to send the audience home satisfied and enriched by the experience; this is achieved by a backstage and front of house partnership where having a team of excellent staff facilitates smooth and efficient stress-free dining.

As a travel journalist I've eaten in hotspots around the world. There have been culinary experiences I will remember forever. A banquet aboard the QE2 as we set sail for New York was one of the most luxurious dining experiences it's possible to have. At the other end of the scale, I had grilled fish and a cold beer on a beach in Malaysia and it cost me about £1.50. If I'd been charged ten times the price it still would have been worth it. However, I have paid through the nose for oysters in Barcelona, knowing full well that they'd been caught on the West Coast of Scotland the day before. I'll never forget eating cockles off a cockle strand in Barra and seeing the lorries being loaded up for the continent with their precious cargo of Scottish seafood.

I always look forward to coming home and having dinner at Gamba. I've even phoned from an airport after an 8 hour flight home and booked myself a table for two later that evening. After 8 hours in the air and awful airline food, there are times of course when the system needs something soothing and plain – simply grilled lemon sole with a glass of Sancerre. Just what the doctor ordered.

In this book you'll find simple dishes that can be prepared after a hard day at the office.
You'll also find more complex combinations of flavours that will impress the most jaded of palates. It's important to stress that although the recipes originated in a restaurant kitchen they are the kind of things you'll want to make at home. This is not a book written to impress other chefs, it's written for people who love great seafood and are looking for fresh ideas to pull together in their own home. The book is divided seasonally and I hope you'll find it easy to use. As well as promoting seasonal availability of ingredients, some dishes are meant to be enjoyed in a particular season. There's not many of us who could handle cod and chips on a hot July afternoon but some dishes like Sashimi Salad have summer written all over them.

The selection of recipes for each season is complimentary and the aim is to make life easy. Each season comes with a complete dinner menu and wine recommendations to take the angst out of making decisions.

If like me you're a Gamba regular then I hope you enjoy re-creating the flavours of your favourite restaurant in your own home. If you've picked up the book and have never dined there, then you've got a treat in store.

Bryan Burnett

Bryan Burnett.

WHERE TO GET IT AND HOW TO USE IT.

Where should I buy my fish?

A decent fishmonger should be your first stop. Sadly, these are pretty few and far between nowadays. If you can find a good one near you then treasure it and get all your friends to support it too. Supermarkets are great for convenience but they are buying huge amounts of fish in bulk so there's not the quality control and personal service that the small guys can provide. And besides there can be few things more unappealing than a pre-packed fillet of fish shrink-wrapped in clingfilm and squeezed into one of those polystyrene trays.

Some of the supermarkets have good wet fish counters where the people staffing them at least know their smokies from their snappers.

The fish at Gamba comes from Andy Bell who has been in the business for twenty-five years. He's recently taken over a retail outlet in the south side of Glasgow although how he finds the time is a mystery, as every morning he's at the fish market at 3.30am in order to select the very best of that morning's catch.

Fish markets where members of the public can shop exist in cities as varied as Stockholm and Sydney. Sadly that doesn't seem to be the case in this country. However, if you happen to find yourself in somewhere like Aberdeen or Peterhead, then a visit to their fish market early in the morning is a tourist attraction in itself.

How can I tell a good fish?

If it smells "fishy" then steer clear. Fresh fish doesn't have a strong smell at all. You might get a slight whiff of the sea but that's about it. It only starts to smell when it starts decomposing. You can tell a lot about a fish by looking into it's eyes (although you might get a few strange glances in the supermarket!). The eyes should be shiny, clear and bright. Also the gills should be bright red. Fillets of fish should be firm to the touch and again shiny and bright.

Shellfish is best bought when alive and kicking although obviously that isn't always possible. Whack it in the fridge as soon as you get it home and cover your fish with clingfilm or a damp cloth. Try to use it the same day as you don't really want it hanging about your fridge for more than 48 hours.

How do I prepare my fish?

The advantage of using a good fishmonger is that he will do all the hard work for you. This gives you the chance to work on the recipe and not be spending your afternoon filleting and boning. Let's face it, how would you rather spend the time? Gutting a fish or guzzling down a gin and tonic? Tough choice!

If you want to get rid of the skin then make sure you've got a really sharp knife. Lay the fish skin side down and angle the knife in at the tail end or thinnest part of the fish and cut between the skin and the flesh to get the knife in. Grab hold of the skin with your hand and pull away at it as the knife slides away from you.

What kind of fish should I buy?

It very much depends on what you're going to do with it. Meaty fish like tuna and swordfish work brilliantly well on the barbeque but would be totally unsuitable for poaching or using in something like a fish pie.

The following are the kinds of fish you'll come across in the recipes in the book. They are not always available at all times of the year, so find out what your fishmonger has in stock before you decide what to cook. I've taken my recipe books out on many a shopping trip and only after I've bought the freshest fish in the shop have I decided what I'm going to do with it.

Lemon Sole

Cooked on the bone and served without much fuss, Lemon Sole is part of a group of flat fish that includes things like Turbot, Plaice and Halibut. Its posh relative, Dover Sole is reckoned by some to have a better flavour but it's expensive enough to put it outside most people's budgets. At Gamba, plain Lemon Sole brushed with butter and served with just a slice of lemon is always on the menu.

Trout (Brown, Rainbow and Sea)

Sea Trout is sometimes known as Salmon Trout and the two fish are remarkably similar. You could certainly use the same cooking methods for both. It's essentially a brown trout that migrates to sea when it's very young. If you are lucky enough to befriend someone who goes fishing they might turn up on your door with a brown trout. You should throw your arms around them and ply them with copious amounts of alcohol as you're getting something very special indeed. Most of the trout we get nowadays is farmed and is known as Rainbow Trout. It's still a good fish but it doesn't have the depth of flavour of it's brown cousin.

Salmon/Wild Salmon

You can buy farmed salmon all year long, but the season for Wild Salmon tends to be between January and August. It tastes better because of its diet and the fact that it gets more exercise from having to swim in strong currents.

There's some pretty poor farmed salmon around but there is good stuff out there as well. The advantage of farmed salmon is that it's made this once luxury item an affordable treat for most people.

Brill

This is a great fish to work with and is suitable for most cooking methods. It's got almost a sweet flavour and although it's in the same group as Sole, its flesh is a bit firmer. It's sometimes referred to as a poor relation of Turbot, which is unfair as it's a perfectly good fish in it's own right. Having said that, if you can't get Turbot (or it's priced out of your budget), then Brill makes a good substitute.

Turbot

Out of all the flat fish, this a favourite. Turbot is generally held up alongside Dover Sole as one of the great flavours in fish cookery but it is priced accordingly. It's a firm, robust fish with incredibly white flesh which will stand up to most cooking methods, and if you feel like splashing out it makes an attractive dinner party dish.

Scallops

The best scallops in the land are to be found off the west coast of Scotland so understandably Gamba makes the most of what's on the doorstep. See p25 for a recipe that brings out their sweet flavour. When it comes to scallops the key is to cook them as briefly as possible. They can be in and out of a frying pan in just 30 seconds each side depending on the thickness. Most fishmongers sell them ready prepared but it isn't that difficult to do yourself. Once you've cleaned it out and removed the "skirt" from around the shell, separate the pink coral from the white fleshy part. A lot of people feel the corals are too soft and mushy to eat with the meaty part but they can be used in sauces.

Halibut

Another firm and meaty fish which can grow to a monstrous size – some have been caught weighing two hundred kilograms. Obviously you won't be buying a whole fish, so it's sold in steaks which are fairly easy to deal with. Just remember to adjust the cooking time for the thickness of the steaks which can vary a lot. You will sometimes see a whole fish for sale. These are baby halibut which are often referred to as "chicken halibut".

Red Snapper

There are hundreds of different varieties of snappers, but the American Red Snapper sits at the head of the snapper family table. Snapper is still considered a fairly exotic fish in this country but in places like Australia it's as common as cod or haddock is here. This is a great fish for cooking whole.

Tuna

When it comes to cafe meals I would take a guess that a baked potato with tuna and mayonnaise has overtaken egg, chips and beans as the nation's favourite – although it's mostly cans of pretty inferior tuna with bucket loads of industrial mayonnaise. Until comparatively recently, fresh tuna was a rarity in this country although it is now widely available. Tuna should always be cooked rare – pink in the middle. If you overcook tuna it turns a horrible grey colour and is fit only for feeding to the cats.

Prawns/Tiger Prawns

Prawns are the nation's favourite crustaceans – Prawn and Mayonnaise sandwiches fly out the door of M&S every lunch-time, Prawn Cocktails have been in and out of fashion more times than flared trousers and then there's the abhorrent but endlessly popular concept of Prawn Cocktail crisps! Most of the prawns sold in supermarkets and fishmongers have already been cooked – so if you are adding them to a dish, do it at the very last moment so they only heat through. Overcooked prawns taste of cotton wool. Not nice! Dealing with uncooked prawns won't present too many problems but you might want to remove the central black vein of larger ones. They will be cooked in under two minutes.

Monkfish

Monkfish are always sold with their heads cut off and one school of thought is that the head is so frightening-looking it would put people off buying the fish. The monkfish has certainly been swallowing the ugly tablets but the real reason it's sold headless is that only the tails are worth eating. Monkfish has become increasingly popular in recent years, especially among people who don't like fish "with bones". Steaks of monkfish tail are readily available and are meaty enough to stand up to some vibrant sauces and cooking methods.

John Dory

Another ugly fish but one that truly proves beauty is only skin deep. A whole fish doesn't give up a great deal of flesh but what you get is well worth the effort and the expense. It's got a great flavour and a firm meaty texture which makes it suitable for nearly all cooking methods. In the recipe on page 81 it's served with prawns and a salsa relish. It's pan fried in the recipe but you could also grill it.

Sea Bream

A wonderful fish for cooking on the bone and if you're going abroad and have asked for a nice bit of grilled fish then chances are it's one of the many varieties of Sea Bream that you've been served. In Spain it's a Dorada and in France it's called a Daurade.

Swordfish

A great many people in this country first tasted swordfish on holiday in the Med where it was simply grilled and served with a slice of lemon and some chips. Now we've really taken to it and in backyards all over Scotland people are slapping another slice of swordfish on the barbie. It works really well on a griddle pan at home and it really stand up to the Cajun spiced prawns in the recipe on p 59. I once had a brilliant fish curry in Malaysia which was made with some succulent swordfish.

Cod

I'm sure there are people who cannot say the word "Cod" without following it up by saying, "with chips". However the versatility of this wonderfully flaky fish is one of the reasons for its enduring popularity. When you're buying cod, look for a really shiny, bright skin. The fillets should be as white as a pint of milk.

Sea Bass

I have seen this fish referred to as aristocratic and it's certainly high up in the pecking order for chefs and food lovers. It's a lovely fish served whole and the skin is really tasty if you can get it nice and crispy. Sea Bass is great stuffed with things like lemon grass, garlic, chilli and ginger.

  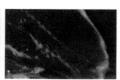  

spring

Tartar of salmon or seatrout
with Sundried Tomato, Crème Fraiche and Basil

SHOPPING LIST

600g salmon or seatrout (raw)
4 sundried tomatoes in oil
2 tbsp crème fraiche
2 spring onions
Basil leaves
Salt and ground white pepper

METHOD

1 Skin and remove all brown pieces of fish.
2 Chop fish to a mince consistency and chill with a little salt and pepper.
   (Do not over salt, as sundried tomatoes are very salty).
3 Chop sundried tomatoes, spring onions, and basil, mix with crème fraiche.
   (Check seasoning, you can add a little pepper, but probably no salt).
4 Mix in with the fish and divide between six chilled glasses, or shape
   in a cutter (2"x2") and place on very cold plates.
5 Ideally serve with wheat wafers or melba toast.

Marinated Sea Trout

with Lime, Ginger and Pink Peppercorns

325g sea trout fillet
juice and zest of three limes
1½ tsp pink peppercorns
15g fresh ginger (grated)
½ tsp salt
1 tsp white sugar

METHOD

1 Using a very sharp knife, slice the raw trout fillets, at right
   angles, towards the tail, very thinly. Place on a tray and chill.
2 Mix all the ingredients together in a bowl and chill, shaking
   every so often to make sure that the juices are mixing.
3 Dip the sliced sea trout in the marinade, lay onto plates, and
   spoon the remainder of the marinade over the fish and serve.

Six Oysters
Roquefort Cream and Toasted Soda Bread

SHOPPING LIST

36 oysters (opened and cleaned)
½ pint fish cream
100g grated roquefort cheese
¼ pint double cream, whipped
1 loaf soda bread

METHOD

1 Place the fish cream in a pan and boil. Remove from heat and add in the
   roquefort, stirring constantly; do not return to heat. Leave to cool slightly.
2 Slice the soda bread and cut in half. Put to one side.
3 Place the oysters on a large tray and heat on the bottom of the grill.
   Add the whipped cream to the roquefort cream and fold in; remove the oysters
   from the grill and spoon on the cream. Toast the soda bread. Put the oysters
   on the top shelf of the grill and colour the cream. Serve with the toast.

Cauliflower, spring onion and shrimp soup

1 medium sized cauliflower
1 onion (sliced)
2 baking potatoes (peeled)
2 cloves garlic
1 bunch spring onions
2 handfuls shrimps (peeled)
3 pts fish stock
salt and ground white pepper
100g butter

METHOD

1 Melt butter in a thick-bottomed pot.
2 While the butter is melting, slice the onion finely and chop the garlic, sweat off in the butter, but do not colour.
3 Divide the cauliflower into florets and add to onion mix; place a lid on the pot and stir for approx. 15 minutes on low heat.
4 Add the fish stock and potatoes and cook on a medium heat, until the potatoes are soft.
5 Slice the spring onions very finely and leave to one side.
6 Liquidise the soup until all the vegetables are pureed. Pass through a sieve and check the seasoning.
7 Before serving add the spring onions, boil the soup and then add the shrimps. Do not re-boil. Serve.

Melon, Prawn and Crab Marie Rose

SHOPPING LIST

3 ogen melons
300g white crabmeat
(frozen or freshly picked)
550g prawns
6 tbsp. Mayonnaise
2 tbsp. Tomato sauce
1 tsp. brandy
½ tsp Tabasco
12 single chives

METHOD

1 Make the marie rose by adding the mayonnaise, tomato sauce, Tabasco and brandy together.
2 Half the melons and remove the seeds. Place in the fridge.
3 Mix the prawns and crabmeat together; bind with a little marie rose so that they are sticking together.
4 Evenly divide the mixture between the melons, and place the remainder of the marie rose on top of the prawn mix in the melons. Place on plates and criss-cross with two chives.

New Potato Salad

with Crab, Parma Ham and Basil Dressing

SHOPPING LIST

400g white crabmeat (frozen or fresh)
600g new potatoes (washed and cooked)
200g Parma ham
6 tbsp. Gamba dressing
8 basil leaves, finely sliced
bunch chives, finely chopped

METHOD

1 Half the potatoes and place in a bowl.
   Mix the basil with the dressing and fold through the potatoes.
2 Slice the Parma ham into one-inch pieces and add to the potato mix.
   Finally add the crabmeat and mix altogether.
3 Divide onto six plates and sprinkle with the chopped chives.

Crisp Fried Sea Trout

with Scallop Cream, Baby Asparagus and Grilled Tiger Prawns

SHOPPING LIST

1 sea trout (2 kilo approx.) or 6 pieces (approx. 300-400g)
18 tiger prawns (shelled and cleaned)
1 bunch baby asparagus (2 if small)
12 scallops (plain, cleaned, out of shell)
1 pint fish stock
½ pint white wine
1 pint double cream
salt and pepper

METHOD

1 Cook asparagus in boiling water until just cooked. Grill tiger prawns under warm grill.
2 Put fish stock in thick-bottomed pan and reduce by half. Add white wine, simmer
   for approx. 5 minutes, add double cream, and season with salt and ground white pepper.
3 Take coral off scallops and add these to boiled cream. Remove from heat; liquidise,
   pass through sieve and leave to one side.
4 Take frying pan with two tablespoons of oil and heat. When smoking add fish skin side
   down and then turn to colour, remove from heat, add scallops to same pan and colour
   on both sides. Remove from pan. Place sea trout under very hot grill to crisp up skin.
5 Place cream mix in pan, add scallops, asparagus and tiger prawns.
6 Equally divide on to 6 warm plates, placing sea trout on top.

salmon Teriyaki

SHOPPING LIST

6 x 180g salmon fillets

FOR THE MARINADE

600ml pineapple juice
300ml sweet soya sauce
40g fresh root ginger
2 tablespoons demerara sugar
3 limes (zest and juice)

METHOD

1 Boil the marinade ingredients together and simmer for approx. 10 minutes.
2 Cool down and marinade salmon for approx. 12 hours in half the teriyaki sauce.
3 Lightly oil a frying pan and fry the salmon presentation side up until pretty dark in colour.
4 Remove the salmon and place under a warm grill.
5 Add the remainder of the teriyaki sauce to the pan and reduce by half.
6 Serve with rice or noodles.

seared scallops
Sweet Beetroot and Pink Peppercorns

SHOPPING LIST

36 x larger scallops
500g fresh beetroot
3 tbsp. redcurrant jelly
1 glass red wine
1 tbsp. pink peppercorns
salt and pepper
3 tbsp. vegetable oil

METHOD

1 Place the scallops on a clean kitchen cloth to soak up any excess water.
2 Grate the beetroot, add two tablespoons oil to a pot, when warm add the
   beetroot and stir.
   After approx. 5 minutes, add the red wine and redcurrant jelly, place a lid on,
   reduce heat and simmer. When this looks sticky add the pink peppercorns,
   a little salt and pepper, stir, remove from heat and keep the lid on.
3 Add the rest of the oil to a frying pan, and while heating, season the scallops.
   When the oil is hot, add the scallops to the pan, making sure you have enough
   space in the pan to turn them round. After a few minutes turn one round to make
   sure it is nice and brown, if so turn all round and colour.
4 Place a tablespoon of beetroot in the centre of the plate, place six scallops
   round the beetroot making sure all the corals are facing the same way.
   Photograph overleaf.

Whole Brown Trout Almandine
with Baby Capers

6 large brown trout gutted and cleaned
150g butter
3 tbsp of flaked almonds
3 tbsp of capers
juice of 2 lemons
chopped parsley

METHOD

1 Put 25g butter in a pan and sauté off the trout on both sides,
   crisping up the skin. Remove from pan and carefully peel off skin and grill.
2 Add remaining 125g of butter to the same pan and melt, reducing the heat.
3 Add almonds, lemon juice, capers and parsley.
4 Pour over the fish and serve.

Goujons of Brill
with Homemade Tartare Sauce

1 brill weighing approx. 2 kilo
(filleted and skinned)
2 cups breadcrumbs
1 cup flour
3 eggs whisked
1 cup good mayonnaise
(or alternatively a 'light' one)
8 gherkins chopped
1 tbsp. baby capers
1 tbsp. chopped parsley

METHOD

1 Cut fillets into strips approx. 10cm in length; roll in flour,
   eggwash and breadcrumbs.
2 Add gherkins, baby capers and parsley to mayonnaise.
3 Fry goujons in very hot oil, serve with half lemon and tartare sauce.

Egg Noodles
with King Prawns, Garlic, Lime and Coriander

SHOPPING LIST

2 pkts egg noodles, blanched for 4 minutes
and cooled in cold water
36 shelled king prawns

SAUCE

1 onion
2 cloves garlic
juice and zest of 6 limes
1 packet coriander
25mls white wine (optional)
2 tsp sugar
1 piece of root ginger or stem ginger grated
500ml of meat stock (see recipe)
4 spring onions

METHOD

1 Sweat off onions, garlic, and ginger, then add lime juice
   and zest, sugar and wine, if wanted.
2 Add stock and reduce further to the proper consistency,
   then blend chopped coriander throughout the sauce.
3 Place wok on heat and when smoking add king prawns,
   cook, then add noodles and heat through.
4 Add lime, garlic and coriander sauce.
   Garnish with spring onions. Serve with chopsticks.

White Chocolate and Pistachio Parfait

SHOPPING LIST

145g white chocolate
60g sugar
2 tbsp water
3 egg yolks
300ml cream
1 pkt pistachio nuts

METHOD

1 Break up white chocolate and place in a blender. Pulse until sandy consistency.
2 Place sugar and water in a thick bottomed pan and boil to 'soft ball' stage*, 120°C.
3 Separate eggs, place egg yolks into a jug, discard whites. Whip up cream until it reaches soft peaks.
4 Turn on blender and pour boiled sugar over white chocolate. Quickly pour egg yolks into mix.
5 Gently fold chocolate mix into semi-whipped cream.
6 Put 12 peeled pistachios into bottom of each of 8 ramekins and top up with the chocolate mix.
7 Freeze for 3 hours; once frozen they are ready to serve with whipped cream and a sprinkling of cocoa powder.

   * 'soft ball' – if unsure please telephone Derek directly at Gamba for an explanation!

Banana, Coconut and Maple Syrup Cheesecake

400g ginger nut biscuits
100g unsalted butter
1kg Philadelphia cheese
200g white chocolate
500ml double cream
30g toasted dessicated coconut
150ml maple syrup
2 bananas (one chopped for cheesecake,
one sliced for caramelising)
sprig of fresh mint

METHOD

1 Melt the butter over a low heat. Place the ginger nuts in a food processor,
   add to the butter and press into the base of a cheesecake tin. Chill for 30 minutes.
2 Whisk the double cream until it reaches the ribbon stage, and chill.
3 Place the Philadelphia in a mixing bowl and beat until soft. Add the chopped banana,
   melted chocolate, maple syrup and coconut. When mixed together, fold in the double
   cream, pour into the cheesecake tin and refrigerate overnight.
4 Unclip the tin and shake it a little until the cheesecake comes away from the edges.
5 With a warm knife, portion the cake into ten pieces, always starting with an equal
   half-moon shape.
6 Take three slices of the second banana and dust with icing sugar, blowtorch
   (or grill), and leave to cool.
8 Dribble some maple syrup on to the bottom of each plate and place a slice
   of cheesecake on top. Arrange the caramelised bananas on top and garnish
   with fresh mint. Photograph overleaf.

Baked Lemon and Rosemary Tart

SHOPPING LIST

9 eggs
380g caster sugar
6 lemons
450ml double cream
3 sprigs rosemary

FOR THE PASTRY

160g plain flour
40g icing sugar
80g butter
1 small whole egg

METHOD

1 Rub flour, butter and icing sugar together till breadcrumb consistency;
   add whole egg to bind breadcrumb mixture together.
2 Rest pastry in fridge for approx. 2 hours.
3 Roll out pastry till approx ½ cm thick all way round.
4 Line tart case with pastry dough and use baking beans for blind-baking.
   Cook for approx. 45 minutes at Gas Mark 3.
5 Remove from oven and remove baking beans. Then cook for a further 15 minutes.
6 Boil cream with fresh rosemary and cool, leave rosemary in the cream to infuse.
7 Cream the eggs and sugar together and add lemon juice and zest.
8 Add the cream to egg mixture and whisk together, pass through sieve into tart case.
9 Cook for approx. 45 minutes at gas mark 3, when the tart is set in centre turn
   oven off and leave for further 15 minutes.
10 Serve with fresh raspberries and clotted cream if preferred.

Dinner Menu

STARTER

Tartar of salmon or seatrout with
sundried tomato, crème fraiche
and basil

MAIN COURSE

seared scallops, sweet beetroot
and pink peppercorns

DESSERT

Banana, coconut and
maple syrup cheesecake

Wine

THE APERITIF: SETTING THE SCENE

A special dinner menu deserves something special by way of introduction, even before the food reaches the table. Wine makes an excellent aperitif, particularly if the menu is based on fish and seafood, as it is here. A light, crisp, dry white wine with enough bite to enliven your guests' taste buds will do the job perfectly. You might like to try a good Muscadet or a flinty French Sauvignon – or perhaps a fresh, unoaked Chardonnay. Sparkling wines are perhaps the best all-rounders, however: from Champagne to Crémant de Bourgogne to Spanish Cava.

STARTER

The combination of smooth, creamy subtlety and tangy, herby piquancy demands a wine of medium body and concentration, with rich but restrained flavours to offset the food. A ripe, rounded, lightly oaked Chardonnay makes a good choice – southern Burgundy excels with these, South Africa too – as will some of Italy's better fish wines, including the smoky Verdicchio. If you absolutely must have red, then go for lighter, low-tannin styles such as good-quality Beaujolais or Pinot Noir. Alternatively, you could opt for a dry, fairly substantial rosé.

MAIN COURSE

Scallops are one of the finer incarnations of seafood, and they deserve a wine to match. Searing intensifies the flavour of the dish and adds a delicious, caramelised note, so you can afford to choose wines with a more assertive character. Again, Chardonnay makes a flattering partner, this time with a touch of toasty oak and creamy richness. For a striking alternative, try a light but incisive Riesling Kabinett from the Mosel – that rapier acidity and trace of delicate sweetness might just provide the perfect foil.

DESSERT

There is one golden rule to remember when choosing wines to drink with dessert: always make sure the wine is at least as sweet as the pudding it accompanies. Sauternes or a botrytised Semillon from, say, Australia would do well with this exotic cheesecake.

mmer

sashimi salad

SHOPPING LIST

Chinese leaves
1 Oak leaf lettuce
sashimi (best fillets of raw fish) of tuna,
swordfish, mackerel (100g of each)
50g julienne of pickled ginger
small handful of pickled ginger
blended with Gamba dressing
Wasabi

WASABI MARINADE

200ml Kikkoman soya
50ml pickled ginger
Tsp. Wasabi (Japanese horseradish)

METHOD

1 Cut fish thinly into 2cm by 1 cm rectangles.
   Skin and remove middle bones from mackerel.
2 Combine marinade ingredients thoroughly and add to fish.
3 Take Chinese leaves and oak leaf and place in a mixing bowl.
4 Add Gamba dressing to dress leaves.
5 Take marinated mixed fish, remove from wasabi marinade.
   Add julienne of pickled ginger.
6 Mix together then serve in a serving bowl and place some
   more marinated fish around the rest of the leaves.

spiced smoked salmon Pot
with Cottage Cheese

SHOPPING LIST

250g smoked salmon
250g cottage cheese
100g Swiss chard leaves*
1 red chilli
½ tsp. cayenne pepper
1 lemon zest and juice
chopped chives

METHOD

1 Combine salmon with lemon juice and zest in blender, pass through a sieve into a bowl.
2 Chop chilli very finely and add along with chives to salmon mix, fold in cottage cheese with cayenne pepper.
3 Spoon into cream pots or ramekins, chill for at least 2 hours.
4 Finish with Swiss chard at side and serve with water biscuits.

*If Swiss chard unavailable use rocket, mustard leaves or little gem lettuce.

Prawn Cocktail

with Straight Malt Whisky

3 egg yolks
3 tsp. white wine vinegar
1 tsp. English mustard
½ tsp. salt
375 ml vegetable oil or olive oil
1 tbsp. Heinz tomato ketchup
1 tbsp. malt whisky
½ tsp. Tabasco
½ tsp. Lea & Perrins
350 g peeled frozen prawns
140 g cos lettuce
1 lemon

METHOD

1 Defrost prawns overnight in fridge.
2 Take a bowl and whisk egg yolks, vinegar, mustard and salt together.
  Continue to whisk and gently pour oil to make mayonnaise.
  Add tomato ketchup, whisky, Tabasco and Lea & Perrins.
3 Finely chop the cos lettuce and divide into six cold glasses;
  place the prawns on top.
4 Pour the sauce over the prawns and serve with a wedge of lemon.

  N.B. If you do not want to make your own mayonnaise,
  ensure you use a good quality one as an alternative.
  Photograph overleaf.

Nicoise salad

300g tinned tuna (soaked in brine)*
300g salad leaves (washed and dried)
6 medium eggs
300g haricot vert (fine green beans)
300g cherry tomatoes
100g pitted black olives
400g boiled new potatoes
100ml Gamba salad dressing
100g mayonnaise

METHOD

1 Boil the eggs in water for 3 minutes and cool under a cold tap.
   Finely grate when the eggs are completely cool.
2 Blanche the beans for 1 minute. Remove and cool in cold water;
   then cut into 1 inch pieces.
3 Cut the boiled potatoes into eight; cut the cherry tomatoes in half,
   removing the eye. Slice the olives finely.
4 Place the lettuce, haricot vert, olives, tomatoes, new potatoes
   and grated egg in a large bowl. Drain tuna and add to the bowl.
5 Whisk the mayonnaise in another bowl and slowly mix in the Gamba
   salad dressing. When finished pour over the other ingredients and mix well.
6 Divide into six bowls making sure it is evenly split.
   Garnish with chopped chive or a sprig of flat parsley.

   *Alternatively make up the salad without the tuna and serve
   with freshly seared tuna (6x50g pieces), instead.

smoked salmon Roulade
with Herbs

SHOPPING LIST

3 shallots, finely chopped
½ tsp. chopped garlic
bunch chives, finely chopped
4 basil leaves, finely chopped
2 sprigs thyme, picked
2 sprigs rosemary, finely chopped
bunch parsley, finely chopped
pinch salt
350g fromage blanc or soft cream cheese
150 g double cream, whipped to soft peak stage
750g sliced smoked salmon (cut length ways)

METHOD

1 Fold the shallots, garlic, herbs and pinch of salt together with the soft cream cheese
   (or fromage blanc), then fold in the double cream and set in the fridge for 2-3 hours.
2 Place the smoked salmon between two pieces of clingfilm and give it a pressing
   with a rolling pin until it is 1 to 2 mm thick. Remove the top layer of clingfilm.
3 Put the cream cheese mix into a piping bag, and pipe a stripe along the leading edge
   of the smoked salmon. Then roll the salmon lightly until you have a near perfect cylinder
   shape. Keep it in the clingfilm and tighten both sides into a knot. Place in the fridge
   and set for 24 hours.
4 Remove the clingfilm and cut the roulade into 12 even pieces. Serve two per person
   with a little mixed salad.

Peppered Tuna steaks
with Tomato and Olive Salad

SHOPPING LIST

2 tbsp. olive oil
2 tbsp. balsamic vinegar
1 dessertspoon cracked black pepper
6 tuna steaks approx. 120g each
3 medium plum tomatoes in wedges
250g pitted black and green olives
100g grilled red peppers in strips
1/3 cup fresh basil chopped
2 tbsp. grilled pine kernels
1 tbsp. Gamba dressing

METHOD

1 Combine oil and balsamic vinegar together, brush over tuna and leave for a few minutes.
2 To make the salad, combine all ingredients together, making sure the eye is out of the tomatoes.
3 Mix with Gamba dressing.
4 Heat a pan till very warm, do not use oil as the dressing on the tuna will do; fry for a few minutes on either side, leaving it pink in the middle; sprinkle one side of fish with pepper.
5 Divide the salad equally onto plates and place tuna on top.

Whole Roast Sea Bream

with Roast Peppers, Chilli Oil and Sweet Soya

SHOPPING LIST

6 sea bream approx. 500-600g
(plain cleaned and scaled)
2 red peppers
2 green peppers
2 yellow peppers
2 red chillies
2 green chillies
¼ pint olive oil
6 tbsp. sweet soya
salt and pepper
3 lemons or limes

METHOD

1 Cut peppers into quarters; grill until the skin goes black. When ready roll in clingfilm or put in a Tupperware dish with lid; this will sweat the peppers. When cool remove the blackened skin.
2 De-seed the chillies and chop very finely, reserve 2 tbsp. olive oil and add chillies with some salt and pepper to the remaining oil.
3 Place two tablespoons in a pan big enough to take two fish. When very warm place the fish in the pan after about 2-3 minutes turn the fish; cook for another 2-3 minutes, remove and place on a baking tray big enough to take all six fish. Cook at Gas Mark 8 for approx. 10 minutes.
4 While the fish are in the oven, slice the skinned mixed peppers; when done mix the peppers with the chilli oil; place under a hot grill to heat through.
5 Take the fish out of the oven and place onto plates. Finally add the sweet soya to the pepper mix, divide the pepper mix between the six fish.
6 Serve with half lemon or lime.

Ginger Grilled Skewered Prawns

with Papaya Salsa

48 fresh tiger or king prawns

FOR THE MARINADE

3 tsp. grated fresh ginger
3 limes zest and juice
1 tbsp. runny honey
1 tbsp. sweet soya sauce
1 tbsp. sesame oil

FOR THE SALSA

2 papaya, peeled, seeded and diced finely
juice of 2 limes
3 tbsp. chopped coriander
1 red chilli finely diced
salt and ground black pepper

METHOD

1 Peel the prawns, cut a slit down the back and pull away any digestive cord if present. Rinse the prawns and pat dry.
2 Place in the bowl with the marinade, chill for 20-30 minutes, tossing every 5-10 minutes.
3 Mix the papaya with the lime juice and coriander. Add the chilli and season.
4 Divide the prawns between six skewers.
5 Preheat a ribbed griddle pan over a high heat or alternatively use a barbecue.
6 Place the prawn skewers onto the heat; as soon as they turn pink turn the over and cook for a further 2-3 minutes.
7 Serve warm or cold with the papaya salsa.

Fillets of Wild Salmon 'Au Poivre'

SHOPPING LIST

6 x 300g pieces of wild salmon
1 tbsp. black pepper cracked
1 tsp. green peppercorns
1 tsp. pink peppercorns
1 onion
200ml of meat stock
500ml double cream
1 measure brandy

METHOD

1 Sweat off onion in a saucepan. Add cracked pepper and a splash of brandy and flame, to burn off the alcohol.

2 Add meat gravy and reduce. Pour in cream and bring to the boil. Reduce, then add pink and green peppercorns.

3 Season salmon. Place on a greased baking sheet and grill for 10-15 minutes.

4 Place salmon on six plates and pour the 'au poivre' sauce around the salmon. Serve with chips or mashed potatoes.

Grilled or Pan-Fried Swordfish

with Cajun Spiced Prawns, Sweet Soya and Lemon

SHOPPING LIST

6 x 200-250g swordfish steaks
olive oil
2 handfuls of prawns
1 tbsp. Cajun spices
3 tbsp. of sweet soya sauce
juice of 2 lemons

METHOD

1 Mix the prawns with the Cajun spices and a little olive oil; marinade for about two hours.
2 Rub the swordfish with olive oil and place on a very warm grill or hot pan and turn after 2-3 minutes. Cook other side as above.
3 Remove the fish and add the prawns to the pan. Sauté them with the sweet soya and lemon juice.
4 Pour over the fish and serve with ½ a lemon.

N.B. Do not add salt to this dish as Cajun spice and sweet soya are both salty.

Whole Lemon Sole Meuniere

1 cup plain flour
6 medium sized lemon sole
125g unsalted butter
6 tbsp. olive oil
salt and ground white pepper
3 lemons
chopped fresh parsley

METHOD

1 Trim lemon sole by removing head, fins and tail. The fishmonger will do this for you whilst he is removing the brown skin.

2 Place the flour on a tray or large plate, sprinkle the fish with salt and pepper. Pat the fish with flour covering completely; shake off excess flour.

3 Heat two tablespoons of oil and $\frac{1}{3}$ of the butter in a large pan, (big enough for two fish), over a medium heat. When it has melted sauté the fish on both sides till golden brown.

4 Remove the fish and place on a baking tray. Add the juice of one lemon to the browned butter, remove from heat and add chopped parsley.

5 Pour butter mix over fish and bake in oven at 180°C for approx. 5 minutes.

6 Garnish with half lemon.

Stewed Rhubarb and Raspberries

SHOPPING LIST

1kg rhubarb
300g raspberries
10ml stem ginger (juice)*
200g granulated sugar

METHOD

1 Take rhubarb and peel to remove red outer skin.
2 Cut rhubarb into 1cm cubes, place in pot with stem ginger and sugar, break down the rhubarb until stewed but watch not to overcook. Remove from heat when rhubarb is still firm.
3 Place rhubarb in glass and place fresh clean raspberries on top.
4 Garnish with mint and serve. (Optionally, serve with ice cream).

*Alternatively use a tbsp grated stem ginger.

Sweet Orange and Poppyseed Cake

SHOPPING LIST

150g self-raising flour
150g caster sugar
30g poppyseeds
6g orange zest
45ml milk
3 medium eggs
180g unsalted butter (melted)

SYRUP GLAZE

90g sugar
75ml orange juice
150ml double cream

METHOD

1   Combine flour, sugar, poppyseeds and orange zest. In another bowl mix milk and eggs.
    Add butter and milk mixture into dry ingredients, mix on a low heat to moisten;
    beat for one minute.

2   Gradually add rest of milk mixture in two additions. Bake in a round spring tin for 1 hour
    at 175°C or Gas Mark 4.

3   To make the syrup glaze, combine sugar and lemon juice and place over low heat
    until sugar has dissolved. Pour hot syrup over hot cake and allow to cool slightly.
    Serve with cream.

Frozen Lemon Curd Yoghurt

SHOPPING LIST

500 ml natural yoghurt (preferably Greek, not set)
350g lemon curd (home-made or good quality bought one)

LEMON CURD

240g caster sugar
juice and grated rind of 2 small lemons
60g butter
3 eggs

METHOD

1 Put sugar and strained lemon juice in pan, partly dissolve, add rind.
2 When quite dissolved add butter and melt.
3 Remove from heat and cool.
4 Beat eggs in a bowl and pour into lemon mixture and cook gently without boiling until thick.

METHOD

1 Gradually stir the lemon curd into the yoghurt until evenly mixed.
2 Pour into container and freeze.
3 Do not stir at all as you would do for ice cream.
4 Remove about 10-15 minutes before serving.

Chocolate Cream
with Grand Marnier*

SHOPPING LIST

115g milk chocolate and
115g bitter chocolate (Bournville)
160ml double cream
160ml milk
1 egg
1 egg yolk
3 tbsp Grand Marnier (or Cointreau)*

METHOD

1 Boil cream and milk.
2 Place chocolate in blender.
3 While blending chocolate add hot cream, milk and eggs and Grand Marnier.
4 Allow to cool. Pass through sieve and pour into ramekins or a mocha cup.
5 Set in fridge overnight.

Dinner Menu

STARTER

Smoked salmon roulade with herbs

MAIN COURSE

Ginger grilled skewered prawns
with papaya salsa

DESSERT

Stewed rhubarb and raspberries

Wine

STARTER

Smoked foods are not always easy to pair with wine, but salmon is a fortunate exception.
The concentration and subtle smokiness of a dry Tokay Pinot Gris from Alsace may be the answer,
although Chablis (or other lightly oaked Chardonnay) and German Riesling Spätlese make equally
good choices. Champagne, of course, is the decadent option. Reds are a possibility, but should
be light.

MAIN COURSE

A bright contrast of flavours and textures, with spicy ginger, delicate prawns and sweet papaya
in a single dish. Choose a dry but fruity white with medium body and preferably no oak - a ripe
Sauvignon Blanc from, say, the Loire Valley or New Zealand, or a zingy, modern Spanish white
from Rueda.

DESSERT

The tang of rasps and rhubarb is best partnered with a sweet wine of matching 'bite', such as
a crisply fruity botrytised or late-harvest Riesling from Germany, Austria, Canada or Australia.

Av

tumn

Fish soup
with Crab Meat, Stem Ginger and Coriander

SHOPPING LIST

275g white fish meat (haddock, cod or whiting)
4 cloves of garlic
50g root ginger
2 medium onions, chopped
50g unsalted butter
3 tbsp. plain flour
1.15 lt. fish stock (see recipe)
1 packet of coriander
50g grated stem ginger
3 tbsp. tomato puree
450g white crabmeat
75ml brandy

METHOD

1 Melt the butter over a low heat in a thick-bottomed pan.
2 Chop the onions, garlic and root ginger, and sweat in a covered pan
   with the butter. Add brandy and reduce.
3 Mix in the flour and cook for about five minutes, still on a low heat.
   Add the tomato puree and keep mixing. Start adding fish stock little by little,
   mixing all the time.
4 Add the white fish meat and cook for 30 to 40 minutes.
5 Liquidise the soup, and pass through a sieve into a clean pot or bowl.
   Add the crabmeat, grated stem ginger and chopped coriander.
6 Serve in warm soup bowls with garlic bread.

salmon Gravadlax

SHOPPING LIST

1kg 200g fresh salmon*
1 large bunch dill (chopped), or 3 tbsp. dried dill
100g sea salt
75g brown demerara sugar
2 tbsp. good brandy

*Ask the fishmonger to cut the middle of the fish;
and cut the salmon lengthways and remove any bones.

METHOD

1 Place half the fish, skin side down onto a large piece of clingfilm.
2 Mix the dill, sea salt, sugar and brandy together.
3 Cover the salmon with the mix and place the other side of salmon on top,
   with skin side up.
4 Wrap the fish in clingfilm and place a weight on top of the fish to press down;
   refrigerate for two days, turning the fish every eight hours, remembering to
   replace the weight every time.
5 Remove the salmon from the brine and slice thinly, like smoked salmon.
   You can scrape off the dill coating, if you like. (I prefer to leave it on).
6 Serve with creamed horseradish or ideally fresh lemon or lime.

Caesar salad

100g Parmesan cheese (shaved)
200g anchovies
500ml mayonnaise
8 slices bread (croutons)
2 cos lettuces

METHOD

1 Take a handful of Parmesan and roughly 12 silver anchovies.
   Place in blender then add mayonnaise to blended mix. Remove to fridge.
2 Remove crust from bread and cut into 1cm square. Place in oven gas mark 4
   and continually keep an eye until golden brown in colour.
3 Take ready prepared cos leaves and place in mixing bowl, add level table spoonful
   of dressing, add anchovies and shaved Parmesan. (Use a potato peeler for shavings).
4 Split into 6 portions or in one large bowl as an accompaniment. Photograph overleaf.

Sweet Pickled Herrings
with Beetroot, Horseradish and Crème Fraiche

SHOPPING LIST

700g raw beetroot, peeled and diced
3 tbsp. horseradish, grated
1 tbsp. creamed horseradish
100g baby spinach or Swiss chard, washed
Gamba dressing to taste
12 sweet pickled herrings
6 tsp. crème fraiche
small bunch chives, finely chopped

METHOD

1 Put the beetroot on to boil; when cooked, drain and allow to cool.
   Then place in a blender and process until very smooth.
2 Add the grated horseradish and creamed horseradish: season to taste
   and place in the fridge.
3 Dress the leaves with dressing and divide among the six plates, arrange
   two herrings on top; place a spoonful of beetroot on top, then add a spoonful
   of crème fraiche at the side and sprinkle with chopped chives.

Sole, Leek and Lobster Terrine

SHOPPING LIST

500g sole fillets
1 small lobster
1 leek finely diced
500ml double cream
2 egg whites
pinch salt

METHOD

1 Fill a large pan, big enough for the lobster, with salted water and bring to the boil. When boiling, place in the lobster and turn off the heat. Leave for 7-8 minutes. Then cool down under running cold water.

2 Once cool, remove the claws, and crack them open using the back of a heavy knife. Prise out the meat then dry off using a clean cloth. Cut the tail length ways and remove the meat; wash off any intestines, then dry. Dice all the lobster meat and put into the fridge until required.

3 Sweat off the leek until soft. Allow to cool and pat off any excess moisture.

4 Switch on the blender adding the sole bit by bit and blitz. Once smooth, pass through a fine sieve into a bowl with the egg whites and stir thoroughly. Little by little pour the cream onto the fish mix, stirring constantly.

5 Mix in the lobster and leek and season. Place the mix into a clingfilm-lined loaf tin or small terrine dish. Place lid on top and cook for 45 minutes at Gas Mark 4.

6 Leave to cool on a cooling tray and refrigerate immediately once cool.

7 Serve with salsa relish (recipe page 81).

John Dory
with Red Pepper, Prawn and Tomato Salsa

SHOPPING LIST

6 fillets of John Dory (approx.) 300-400g
2 red peppers
6 plum tomatoes
2 red chillies
2 handfuls peeled prawns
1 tbsp. caster sugar
1 bunch of coriander
1 red onion - sliced
½ glass of white wine
1 tbsp. of oil

METHOD

1 Quarter peppers, grill until skins are blackened, put in Tupperware to sweat until cold. Put to one side.
2 Put on a pan of water and bring to the boil. Remove the eye from tomatoes and criss cross opposite end. Blanche in water for a few seconds and immediately put into ice cold water. Remove skin from tomatoes and peppers. Dice. Finely chop chilli.
3 Slice onion thinly; sweat off in oil. Do not colour. Add sugar, chillies and white wine. Remove from heat and mix through tomatoes and peppers and chopped coriander. Put in a bowl; add prawns and chill; stir occasionally.
4 Sear John Dory on both sides on a griddle pan or a very warm frying pan and place on top of salsa.

Seared Halibut

with Baby Onion, Mussels and Saffron Stew

SHOPPING LIST

4 halibut fillets (about 150-175g)
24 small onions (the smaller the better)
1 clove of garlic
20g butter
1-2g saffron strands
2 tbsp. chives
200ml white wine
200ml fish stock
200ml double cream
200g mussel meat
(either buy fresh from fishmonger
or tinned from supermarket)

METHOD

1   Slowly melt the butter in a pan, add the whole baby onions and garlic,
    and sweat until the onions colour lightly, then remove them.
2   Add the white wine to the pan and reduce by half, then add the fish stock
    and simmer. Add the double cream and reduce further.
3   Place a frying pan on quite a high heat with a little vegetable oil.
    When it starts to smoke, add the halibut, presentation side first,
    and reduce the heat. When slightly brown, remove from the pan
    and place on the bottom half of the grill.
4   Add the mussel meat to the cream sauce, along with the saffron and onions.
5   Take the mussels and onions out of the sauce with a perforated spoon,
    and place them in the centre of a flat pasta plate. Place the halibut on top.
6   Add chives to the sauce, pour a little on the plate and serve.

Lobster Thermidor

6 lobsters weighing 1lb/500g each
1 litre double cream
1 onion
250g Cheddar cheese grated
250g Parmesan grated
1 measure brandy
1 tbsp English mustard

METHOD

1 Place lobsters in a pan of boiling water and turn off immediately.
   Leave to sit for 5-10 minutes then cool down under cold water.
2 Dice onion and sweat off in a small saucepan, flame with brandy,
   then add mustard and $^3/_4$ litre of double cream. Bring to the boil.
3 Once boiled remove from heat and whisk in Parmesan and cheddar.
4 Once the lobster are cooled and drained, cut in half, length wise.
   Wash away any intestines.
5 Break off claws and crack open. Remove all meat from claws.
6 Take the tail out of the shell and dice with the claw meat.
   Place the diced lobster into the empty shells.
7 Whisk the remainder of cream and add to warm sauce.
8 Heat the lobster under the grill until hot, or place in hot oven
   to heat through.
9 Place lobster halves on oval plates. Pour over the thermidor sauce
   and glaze under the grill.
   Photograph overleaf.

Prawn Linguini

with Sundried Tomatoes, Chilli Oil, Rocket and Parmesan

SHOPPING LIST

600g pre-cooked fresh linguini
2 cloves garlic chopped
1 tsp. chopped red and green chilli
24 raw king prawns, peeled, de-veined and sliced lengthways
bunch chopped chives
6 basil leaves, chopped
150g rocket, picked and washed
24 Halved sundried tomatoes (in oil)
salt and ground pepper
8 tbsp extra virgin olive oil

METHOD

1 Put three tbsp. olive oil in a pan and heat slowly. Add the garlic
  and fresh chilli; slowly heat to release the flavours. Do not burn.
2 Add the prawns and cook for approx. 30 seconds, stirring constantly.
  Add the chopped herbs, making sure the ingredients are not sticking
  to the pan. Add the rocket and let wilt slightly.
3 Place the pre-cooked pasta into the pan, mixing well with the prawns.
  Add the sundried tomatoes and mix together.
4 Season with salt and pepper, remembering the sundried tomatoes
  are salty.
5 Divide into six bowls and serve with fresh Parmesan.

Thai Fish Cakes

with Sweet Thai Jelly

SHOPPING LIST

900g potatoes
400g salmon fillets
400g crabmeat
200g chopped prawns
1½ tsp chilli oil
1 bunch coriander (chopped)
2 limes, zest and juice
salt and ground white pepper
3 tbsp. plain flour
2 eggs
1 cup breadcrumbs

FOR THE THAI JELLY

350g apple jelly
2 clove garlic
1 red chilli
1 green chilli
juice of 3 limes
1 small bunch coriander
2 balls stem ginger grated

METHOD

1 Peel and cook potatoes; mash when ready.
2 Cook the salmon in the oven or grill, mash together with crabmeat and chopped prawns, mix in the chilli oil, coriander, lime zest and juice, salt and pepper. Add to potato mixture.
3 Shape into a round shaped cutter approx. 3in in diametre, chill for approx. 1 hour.
4 Put flour on a plate or tray and dust fishcakes, then put in beaten eggs and finally coat with breadcrumbs.
5 Fry in knob of butter and 2 tbsp. olive oil; or deep fry in a frying pan.
6 Blend or liquidise all ingredients for Thai jelly; return to jar and chill.
7 Serve fishcakes on warm jelly with mixed salad or bamboo shoots.

(This could be used as a starter using half the recipe quantities).

scallops and Monkfish
En Papillotte

8 pieces of greaseproof paper cut to size of your plate
16 scallops
2 monkfish tail; cut into 16 pieces
8 spring onions
60g fresh root ginger
1 tsp. demerara sugar
juice of 1 lemon
2 tbsp sweet soya sauce

METHOD

1 Lightly grease the paper with oil.
2 Sweat ginger in a little oil on the stove, add brown sugar and stir, add lemon juice
   and sweet soya. Take off gas and mix in spring onions, do not cook.
3 Place scallops and monkfish alternately on piece of greaseproof paper; season with salt.
4 Sprinkle ginger and spring onion mix on top with a little juice.
5 Place another piece of greaseproof paper on top and fold sides in order to overlap tightly.
6 Cook in oven on greased tray at gas mark 8, until greaseproof paper rises, which indicates
   that the fish is cooked.
7 Serve straight out of the oven, as fish will continue to cook in the paper.

This is a very quick way to cook fish. Photograph overleaf.

Fruit and Nut Chocolate Custard

SHOPPING LIST

275ml double cream
275 ml milk
170g dark chocolate
170g milk chocolate
50g hazelnuts
50g sultanas
50g raisins
2 eggs
50g sugar

METHOD

1 Boil milk and cream in a thick-bottomed pan.
2 Separate eggs and place yolks in a bowl with sugar, whisk until white.
3 Add milk chocolate and dark chocolate to the cream and milk mixture pour over the eggs whisking constantly.
4 Sieve into a large jug and skim off froth.
5 Grill hazelnuts until dark and rub between two clean cloths to remove skin.
6 Place the peeled hazelnuts, raisins and sultanas into the ramekins.
7 Top up the ramekins with the chocolate custard and cook in a bain marie at gas mark 3/160°C for 40 minutes.

Auntie Mary's Carrot Cake

SHOPPING LIST

1½ cup self raising flour
4 grated pieces of stem ginger
1¼ cup caster sugar
¾ cup olive oil
½ cup sultanas
2 cups grated carrot
1 tsp. Baking powder
2 tsp. Ground cinnamon
2-3 eggs

METHOD

1 Sieve flour, baking powder and cinnamon in a large bowl.
2 Add sugar, sultanas, stem ginger and carrots to the flour mix.
3 Whisk eggs and add olive oil and pour onto the dry ingredients. Mix well.
4 Grease and flour a 1lb loaf tin, pour mixture into the tin and cook
   for 1hour at 160°C/gas mark 4.
5 Serve hot with crème fraiche or vanilla ice cream.

Poached Pears

with Marsala, Cinnamon and Cloves

SHOPPING LIST

6 firm pears
1 pint red wine
½ pint Marsala wine
1 cinnamon stick
2 cloves
240g caster sugar

METHOD

1 Peel the pears leaving the stems on. Put in a pan with the wines, sugar, cinnamon stick and cloves. Bring to the boil; turn down to a simmer and cover with a lid.
2 Poach the pears gently for 40-45 minutes, then cool in the liquid.
3 When cold, remove the pears and return the poaching liquor to a fast boil, reducing by half. Allow this syrup to cool, then return the pears to it.
Coat the pears with the syrup and leave to soak overnight.
4 Ideally serve with ice-cream or pouring cream.

Dinner Menu

STARTER

Fish soup with crabmeat, stem ginger
and coriander

MAIN COURSE

John Dory with red pepper, tomato
and prawn salsa

DESSERT

Poached pears with Marsala,
cinnamon and cloves

Wine

STARTER

A glass of bone-dry manzanilla or fino sherry might well be the best choice for this oriental-style soup, but aromatic Sauvignon Blanc comes a close second.

MAIN COURSE

The fine-flavoured John Dory merits a full-bodied, classic Chardonnay, especially Burgundy or top Californian wines. There are other options, however. Sauvignon Blanc will echo the flavours of red peppers and tomatoes, whilst juicy, low-tannin reds provide an interesting alternative with any fish.

DESSERT

A glass of Marsala is the obvious accompaniment to this distinctive dessert. However, you may like to try one of Italy's sweet Moscatos, or even sparkling Asti, as a lighter alternative.

vinter

Potato, Leek and Mussel soup

SHOPPING LIST

3 large leeks
3 baking potatoes
1 onion
2 litres fish stock
500g mussels
1 bay leaf
crème fraiche
2 cloves garlic

METHOD

1 Slice leeks finely and wash thoroughly. Dice onion and potatoes.
2 Sweat off leeks, onions, garlic and potatoes in a thick bottom pan until soft.
3 Add fish stock and boil, cook until potatoes are soft.
4 Clean and pick mussels ensuring there are no beards. Place in a pan
  with a tight fitting lid, cook until open. When cool remove the mussels
  from their shells.
5 Blend the soup, pass through a sieve and check seasoning.
6 Heat the soup and add mussels with a dollop of crème fraiche.

Steamed Oban Mussels

with Red Curry, Coconut and Coriander

3 kilos mussels, cleaned and de-bearded
1 large onion, sliced
1 tsp. red curry paste
1 glass white wine
1 tin coconut milk
1 tbsp. desiccated coconut
bunch coriander, chopped
salt

METHOD

1. Put onion, mussels and wine in a pot with lid, put on high heat until all mussels open.
2. Remove mussels and separate into bowls; to the remaining liquor add curry paste, coconut milk, coconut and a little salt, reduce by half, add coriander, pour over mussels.
3. Serve with garlic bread.

Peppered Mackerel Cheesecake

625g peppered mackerel
125g cream cheese
¼ pint cream
1 whole lemon
¼ tsp. paprika
¼ tsp. cayenne
150g oatcakes
50g butter
1 egg white

METHOD

1. Blend oatcakes until fine.
2. Melt butter and add to oatcakes.
3. Place the oatcakes in the base of a 6-8 inch spring loaded cheesecake tin and refrigerate.
4. Remove skin and brown flesh in the centre of the mackerel fillets.
5. Place in a food processor, add the cream cheese, lemon juice, paprika and cayenne.
6. Place in a large mixing bowl and slowly fold in cream and egg white.
7. Pour into cheesecake tin and set in fridge overnight. Serve with crème fraiche and rocket leaves with Gamba dressing.

seared scallops
Chinese Cabbage, Smoked Bacon and Sesame Seed Dressing

SHOPPING LIST

24 larger scallops (cleaned)
4 rashers smoked bacon
(cut into thick strips)
2 Chinese cabbages
Gamba dressing for 6
1 tbsp. black sesame seeds
1 tbsp. natural sesame seeds
1 tbsp. sesame oil
salt
1 tbsp vegetable oil

METHOD

1 Break up Chinese cabbage and wash thoroughly; let drip dry in a colander.
2 Pat dry the scallops to soak up any water.
3 Heat the oil in a frying pan; when it is smoking add the bacon and fry till dark in colour, making sure you move it around constantly. When browned remove from pan and leave to one side.
4 Mix the sesame seeds and sesame oil with the Gamba dressing. Give the leaves a good shake and put into a mixing bowl, pour over the sesame dressing and divide between six plates.
5 Using the same pan as the bacon was fried in, return it to the heat, reducing the heat add the scallops and salt very lightly; colour scallops and scatter the bacon over them evenly. This is a delicious combination of flavours.

Feuilletté of lobster

Asparagus, Mussels and Thyme Fish Cream

SHOPPING LIST

350g puff pastry
1 large lobster
6 handfuls of mussels (de-bearded and cleaned)
1 bunch asparagus
3 sprigs fresh thyme
fish cream for six
1 egg yolk

METHOD

1. Put lobster into boiling water, turn heat off and leave lobster in; when it turns orange run under cold water; when cool remove from water. Take meat out of shell and chop into bite size pieces. Place in the fridge.
2. Place mussels in a pan with a little water. Cover with a lid and cook on a high heat until all are opened. Keep the lid on until the mussels are cool.
3. Cook the asparagus in boiling water. Cool under cold water and drain; cut into pieces about 1½ inches in length. Put in the fridge.
4. Roll out the pastry to approx. 1cm thick; criss-cross the top of the pastry with a fork. Cut the pastry with a cutter approx. 7cm in diameter. Brush with egg yolk. Cook in oven at Gas Mark 5 on a greased tray for approx. 20 minutes until golden brown. Remove and cool on a cooling tray.
5. Bring the fish cream to the boil; add the thyme, lobster, mussels and asparagus.
6. Slice the feuillettées into three. Divide the lobster mix evenly between the layers of pastry, putting the top criss-crossed piece on last.

Fillets of Turbot

with Sorrel Cream, Oysters and Salmon Ketta

SHOPPING LIST

6 fillets of turbot approx. 180g each in weight
18 oysters (opened and chilled)
fish cream for six
6 sorrel leaves medium size
4-6 tsp. salmon ketta (fish eggs)
2 tbsp. vegetable oil
salt

METHOD

1 Flour the turbot fillets and leave to one side.
2 Heat the fish cream in a saucepot, slowly bringing to the boil; when boiled add the sorrel and simmer on a very low heat.
3 Fry the fillets of turbot in a pan, making sure the pan is hot. You want to colour the turbot on one side making sure it's lightly browned, place on a baking tray under the grill for approx. 5 minutes.
4 Remove sauce from stove and add the oysters, do not re-boil as the oysters will go rubbery and taste horrible.
5 Divide the sauce between the six plates, placing the turbot on top; to finish place the ketta on top of the turbot and serve.

N.B. If ketta is unavailable you could use cod or herring roe but they may discolour.

Grilled Monkfish
with Leeks, Honey and Mustard Glaze

SHOPPING LIST

3 medium sized prepared monkfish tails (each to serve 2 people)
2 medium size leeks
600ml fish stock
½ a 280g jar clear honey
2 dessertspoons English mustard
2 dessertspoons French mustard
2 dessertspoons Dijon mustard
2 dessertspoons grain mustard
Knob of butter
Salt and pepper

METHOD

1 To start put the fish stock on to reduce by half, when reduced add the honey
   and mustard and reduce by about ³/₄. Leave to one side when done.
2 The fishmonger should prepare your monkfish tail for you, if not then remove
   from the bone and skin completely. Cut into six equal portions.
3 Butter a grilling tray big enough to fit the monkfish on, brush the monkfish with butter on,
   and place on the bottom of the grill.
4 Wash and cut leeks about one inch in length, wash again as dirt will get inside layers,
   let drip in a colander or dry with kitchen roll.
5 Place the butter in a thick bottomed pan, when melted add the leeks and sauté
   with little salt and pepper, turn heat down and cook leeks, but do not colour.
6 The fish should take approx. 10-15 minutes to cook through, when ready
   place the leeks in the centre of the plate, put the monkfish on top and finish
   with the mustard glaze. This is very strong so a little is all you need.

Smoked Haddock

with Black Pudding Mash and Syboes

SHOPPING LIST

6 fillets smoked haddock
4 large potatoes
3 slices black pudding
1 bunch syboes (spring onions)
1 pint basic fish cream
1 pint milk
knob of butter
salt and ground white pepper

METHOD

1 Put potatoes on to boil and fry black pudding or grill, the healthier choice.
2 Pour milk into a deep tray and slowly bring to the boil, add the haddock and turn gas off.
3 Slice spring onions and fry in butter, add one ladle of milk from the haddock tray
   and reduce, add cream with a little salt and pepper. Simmer on a low heat.
4 Mash potatoes and black pudding together and divide equally by 'quennelling' onto plates;
   place smoked haddock fillet on top and pour cream around. Photograph overleaf.

Risotto of Lobster
Asparagus, Crème Fraiche and Chive

480g risotto rice (arborio or carnaroli)
1 onion, finely chopped
2.25 litres good fish stock
45g butter
2 cloves garlic, chopped
22g grated Parmesan
tbsp. olive oil
1 good sized lobster
1 bunch asparagus
6 dessertspoonfuls crème fraiche
1 bunch chives chopped
salt and ground white pepper

METHOD

1   Cook the lobster in boiling water, turn the heat off when lobster has been put in and leave for approx. 5 minutes; run under cold water to cool.

2   Divide the stock between two pans, bring to the boil. Add the whole asparagus to one pan and boil for 2-3 minutes, remove asparagus and cool in cold water immediately. Cut into 1 inch sized pieces.

3   Place the olive oil in a pan; fry the onion and garlic, cook until soft. Add the butter to the onions and garlic, then add the rice, making sure it's thoroughly coated in the butter and oil, fry for a few more minutes, then stir in two ladles of the fish stock, keep stirring regularly, adding more stock as the rice absorbs the liquid.

4   Remove all the lobster meat from the shell and dice into decent size pieces.

5   Add the remainder of the stock slowly to rice, after 20-25 minutes the rice will have absorbed all the stock and the rice should have a slight bite to it.

6   Stir in the Parmesan, asparagus, lobster and chives; season to taste and serve immediately with a dollop of crème fraiche on top.

smoked salmon omelette
with Watercress Cream

SHOPPING LIST

12 eggs
300g smoked salmon
6 tbsp. olive oil
600ml fish stock
300ml white wine
600ml double cream
1 bunch watercress
½ tsp. salt
½ tsp. white pepper

METHOD

1 Whisk eggs together and chill.
2 Put white wine in a thick-bottomed pan and reduce by half. Once reduced add fish stock and reduce by half again. Add double cream, bring to the boil slowly, add chopped watercress and simmer for approx 10 minutes.
3 Remove sauce from heat and liquidise; pass through a sieve and return to a very low heat.
4 Heat omelette pan and when very warm add tablespoon of olive oil. Swirl round and add enough omelette mix for one. Keep moving mix around with fork and when starting to cook, cover bottom of pan and add smoked salmon. Fold omelette over and place onto plate. Cover with sauce and serve.

N.B. if using for a starter please use a small bilini pan.

Fillets of Rainbow Trout
with Black Bean Butter Sauce

SHOPPING LIST

6 x rainbow trout, filleted skinned and pin boned
125g unsalted butter
Flour for dusting
3 lemons
½ cup white wine
2 tbsp. dried black beans
1 tbsp. sweet soya
1 tbsp. olive oil
Pinch of salt

METHOD

1 Heat oil in pan. Lightly dust trout fillets with flour. Fry the fillets in the pan until lightly browned.
2 Melt ⅓ of the butter in the same pan, add the sweet soya, black beans and wine.
3 Bring the wine to the boil, turn heat down, reduce by half, add the remainder
   of the chilled butter, constantly moving pan always, making sure the sauce
   does not curdle.
4 Pour over the fillets and garnish with half lemon. Photograph overleaf.

Rum and Raisin Crème Brûlée

SHOPPING LIST

360ml double cream
360ml milk
7 egg yolks
105g granulated caster sugar
½ vanilla pod (or vanilla essence 1 tsp.)
3 tbsp. raisins
2 tbsp. dark rum

METHOD

1. Mix rum and raisins together; chill overnight in fridge
2. Place egg yolks and caster sugar in bowl; whisk together until smooth.
3. Bring milk and cream to boil with split ½ vanilla pod.
4. Pour milk mixture onto egg mix and whisk constantly.
5. Divide raisin mix between six ramekins.
6. Skim brûlée mix making sure no froth is on top of mix.
7. Pour over raisins into ramekins, cook in oven gas mark 3, 160°C for 35-45 mins.
8. Cool down and chill for about 4-6 hours.
9. Before serving sprinkle with granulated sugar and glaze under a very warm grill or alternatively with a blowtorch.

Strawberry Hearts

SHOPPING LIST

300g butter
155g sugar
450g plain flour

FOR FILLING

300g strawberries
200g mascarpone
50g icing sugar

COULIS

4 tsp. water
300g raspberries
100g sugar
(Boil raspberries and sugar; reduce and pass through a sieve.)

METHOD

SHORTBREAD

1 Cream butter and sugar together. Add sieved flour and bind together.
   Place in fridge to rest for approx. 30 minutes.
2 Roll out pastry 1cm thick and cut with a heart shaped cutter. Cook at gas mark 3
   for 20 minutes; sprinkle with caster sugar when removed from oven.
3 Quarter all strawberries removing stalks. Take mascarpone and mix sieved
   icing sugar together.
4 Place bottom of shortbread fixed with a little mascarpone to hold in place.
5 Take some mascarpone; mix and spread on bottom.
6 Layer then cover with strawberries and top with another layer of shortbread.
   Dust with icing sugar. Dribble coulis around shortcake.

Rice Pudding
with Strawberry Jam

6 tbsp of strawberry jam or conserve
300g pudding rice
3 tbsp caster sugar
½ small tin condensed milk (218g tin)
1 litre milk

METHOD

1 Wash pudding rice in a sieve under cold running water to remove starch.
2 Place in a medium size pot with milk, sugar and condensed milk, cook on a low heat
   for about half an hour stirring regularly to avoid rice sticking.
3 Remove from heat, transfer to a deep oven dish and bake in oven gas mark 3
   until a skin is formed. Serve with a generous helping of strawberry jam or conserve.

Dinner Menu

STARTER

Feuilletté of lobster, asparagus, mussels
and thyme fish cream

MAIN COURSE

Grilled monkfish with leeks, honey
and mustard glaze

DESSERT

Rum and raisin crème brûlée

Wine

STARTER

Served on its own, the noble lobster is often paired with fine, full-bodied white wines from the classic areas of Burgundy and Bordeaux. As part of a feuilletté, however, there is scope for a wider range of wine styles, although quality remains a must. A top-notch Sauvignon Blanc from the Loire or from New Zealand's Marlborough district will complement the asparagus and thyme components of the dish, whilst a rich but subtle Pinot Gris from Alsace – or indeed any wine of substance made from one of the less assertively flavoured grape varieties – will provide an elegant backdrop.

MAIN COURSE

The firm flesh of monkfish will easily stand up to a full-bodied, flavoursome white wine, such as fine Burgundy or one of the more restrained Chardonnays from California or South Africa. Red wine is also a possibility – Pinot Noir is a particularly good choice – but you may find that the inherent sweetness of the leek and honey glaze accompaniment directs you more easily towards white wines. As an alternative to Chardonnay, try Viognier (Condrieu is its top incarnation) or a herby, savoury white wine from the Rhône.

DESSERT

A sweet Muscat is probably the best choice with the rum and raisin flavours of this crème brûlée, but be careful to err on the light side. The sweet, sparkling Italian version, Asti (spumante), makes a surprisingly good choice at the end of a rich meal.

Gamba

Favourites

Crab and sweetcorn soup

SHOPPING LIST

1 large onion
2 cloves garlic
125 g soft butter
3 tbsp plain flour
2 litres fish stock
1 tbsp soya sauce
1 medium tin sweetcorn
500 g fresh white crabmeat

METHOD

1 Chop the onion and garlic.
2 Melt the butter in a thick bottomed pan, sweat off the onion till soft, do not colour.
3 Add flour and cook for 5 mins without colouring.
4 Slowly add fish stock and cook for about thirty minutes, reduce heat and simmer for a further ten minutes.
5 Add half tin sweetcorn and liquidize, pass through a sieve into clean pot.
6 Add soya sauce, remainder of sweetcorn and season with salt and pepper, finally add crabmeat and bring to the boil. Serve with garlic bread (optional).
7 Soup always tastes better 2/3 days after making; this enables all the flavours to come through more.

smoked salmon, spinach, Goat's Cheese and Caper salad
with Sesame Dressing

200 g smoked salmon cut into strips
200 g goat's cheese
200 g spinach leaves
1 tbsp capers
sesame dressing
(use Gamba house dressing with the addition of toasted sesame seeds
and sesame oil. About one dessert spoon of each.)

METHOD

1 Put spinach and smoked salmon in a large mixing bowl and fold through with hands.
2 Crumble in the goat's cheese using fingers; add capers and sesame dressing; fold further with hands.
3 Divide salad between six bowls and serve.
4 There is no salt or pepper needed as capers and smoked salmon are rather salty.

scallop salad
with Lemon Grass and Parmesan Shavings

SHOPPING LIST

150 g rocket leaves
150 g spinach
1 lollo rosso (picked)
36 large scallops
2 tbsp Gamba salad dressing
500 g parmesan for shaving
salt and pepper

FOR LEMON GRASS DRESSING

250 g Apple jelly
1 bunch lemon grass
2 cloves garlic
1 red chilli
juice 3 limes
2 balls of stem ginger

METHOD FOR LEMON GRASS DRESSING

Heat apple jelly in pan with all other ingredients, except for the lemon grass, on a low heat. Peel outer shell of lemon grass and chop very finely. When all the ingredients have dissolved in the jelly, remove from heat and add lemon grass and liquidize. Leave to cool, then pass through a sieve.

METHOD

1 Wash all leaves and dry in a salad spinner. Place in a bowl and add Gamba salad dressing, salt and pepper. Mix with hand and divide between six bowls.
2 Add a tablespoon of vegetable oil to a frying pan; when smoking add scallops and colour for 1-2 minutes on either side.
3 Remove and arrange on dressed leaves and with a potato peeler shave the parmesan over the salad.
4 Lightly dribble lemon grass dressing over the whole salad; this will be quite strong in flavour so only a little will be required.

Fresh Crab, Avocado and Pink Grapefruit

SHOPPING LIST

200 g fresh crab (white meat preferably)
2 ripe avocados
2 pink grapefruit (segmented)
200 g rocket
4 tbsp Gamba dressing
Maldon sea salt
pepper

METHOD

1 Rub crab through fingers and check there is no shell in it.
2 Place crab in a bowl with chopped avocado, leave avocado quite large, and add grapefruit segments and rocket.
3 Combine all ingredients with Gamba dressing and season with salt and pepper.
4 Serve in bowls with crusty bread or pitta bread.

Pressed Salmon and Horseradish Terrine

SHOPPING LIST

400 g salmon
100 g smoked salmon chopped
1 tbsp horseradish creamed
1 blanched onion
1 tsp pink peppercorns
zest and juice 2 lemons
salt and pepper

METHOD

1 Poach the salmon in ½ litre of water with lemon juice and zest, onion and pink peppercorns.
2 When cooked, remove salmon from water and pour the water through a sieve, keeping the onions, zest and peppercorns.
3 Flake salmon into a bowl; add onions, zest, and peppercorns with creamed horseradish. Season with salt and pepper.
4 Line a terrine with cling film and press salmon mix into it, refrigerate overnight pressing salmon mix down with a weight.
5 Remove from terrine and slice; this may be a bit crumbly but when saving press together.
6 Serve with warm toast.

Whole Roasted Sea Bass
with Herb Gravy, Orange and Shrimps

SHOPPING LIST

6 sea bass cleaned and scaled
1 quantity of meat stock (see page 149)
3 oranges
1 small bunch rosemary
1 bunch thyme, mint, basil, coriander, chives and chervil (all chopped)
1 kilo peeled shrimps
salt and pepper
2 tbsp redcurrant jelly or mint jelly

METHOD

1. Place meat stock in a pot and reduce. Add redcurrant jelly or mint jelly and when reduced by half, add all the chopped herbs; leave off the gas and let herbs infuse the stock. Leave for ten minutes. Liquidise and pass through a sieve into a pan (not a pot).
2. Season your sea bass on both sides. In a pan heat some oil, and when hot add two sea bass at a time, cooking for 3-4 minutes either side, then take off heat and place on a baking tray that will take all six fish. Repeat until all fish are fried and on the baking tray.
3. Cook in a hot oven for approx. 10 minutes.
4. While fish are cooking, peel oranges and segment. Always make sure that oranges have been 'top and tailed' ensuring you always have a flat side. When taking skin off with a knife, segment orange making sure no pith is left on the segments, as this is very bitter.
5. When sea bass are cooked, place on warm plates, reheat herb gravy and bring to the boil. Add orange segments and peeled shrimps. Take off heat and divide sauce between the fish. (Do not reboil with shrimps in it, as they will go rubbery).

Grilled Halibut
with Sweet Pepper Cream and Pesto

SHOPPING LIST

6 pieces halibut fillets
1 chopped onion
2 red peppers chopped
2 cloves garlic chopped
1 tbsp granulated sugar
200ml white wine
200ml fish stock
200ml double cream
salt and pepper

FOR PESTO

1/2 kilo pine kernels
4 cloves garlic
200ml extra virgin olive oil
100 g grated parmesan
1 large bunch of basil
salt and pepper

METHOD FOR PESTO

Add pine kernels, garlic and parmesan to Robot Coupe with the basil, liquidize for a short time and add olive oil slowly. When all ingredients are pureed, season to taste.

METHOD

1 Sweat off onion and garlic in a little butter, add chopped red pepper and sweat off until cooked, but do not colour. Add sugar and white wine.
2 Reduce the white wine till nearly all reduced into pepper mix; add fish stock and do the same.
3 When both liquids are reduced add the cream and bring to the boil, take off and liquidise, pass through a sieve into a clean saucepot, bring to the boil and season to taste. Place to one side.
4 Grease a tray big enough to take six pieces of halibut. Place halibut on the tray and brush with oil or melted butter. Cook on top of grill until a bit of colour appears on the fish. When done, put on bottom part of grill or in a hot oven, cook for 3-5 minutes and then place on warm plates.
5 Put about one tsp of pesto on top of fish and put under grill for 30 seconds just to take the chill off the pesto.
6 Pour sweet pepper sauce round fish and serve.

Mussel stew

with Asparagus, Thyme and Oysters

300 g mussel meat
2 bunches of asparagus cooked using only the upper-tipped half
2 sprigs thyme
12 oysters
1 onion finely sliced
salt and pepper
1 quantity of fish cream (see page 148)

METHOD

1. Sweat off finely sliced onion in a pan but do not colour.
2. Add thyme and fish cream, bring to the boil and add mussel meat.
3. Cut the asparagus in half and add to mussel stew.
4. Open oysters and divide between six bowls, before putting stew in. Do not boil the oysters as this will toughen them and make them rubbery.
5. Before serving give a quick flash under a very warm grill.

Organic salmon
with Potato, Pea, Mussel and Red Pepper Stew

SHOPPING LIST

6 pieces organic salmon (approx. 300-400 g)
300 g mussel meat
12 small new potatoes cooked and sliced
3 tbsp petit pois
2 red peppers diced small
fish cream (recipe page 148)

METHOD

1 Take the organic salmon and fry in a pan in hot oil, skin side down. When crispy turn over and cook for a further 3-4 minutes, remove from the pan and place on a baking tray.
2 Put fish cream in a pot with the mussels, sliced new potatoes and diced red pepper; bring to the boil and remove from heat, add peas at last minute as they will discolour.
3 Put salmon in a hot oven for approx. 5 minutes until heated through; divide stew between six bowls and heat under grill for one minute. Place salmon on top and serve.

seared Turbot
with Browned Lemon Butter and King Prawns

6 pieces of meaty turbot
18 king prawns shelled and halved
125 g unsalted butter
1 large lemon
Maldon sea salt
cracked pepper
bunch chives (chopped)

METHOD

1 Heat a large frying pan big enough to bake six pieces of turbot. When very hot add a little oil.
2 When oil is smoking slightly reduce heat and place seasoned turbot in pan with the rounded side down first. Cook for 3-4 minutes, colouring the fish to a brown colour; when done, remove the fish from the pan and place on a baking tray, browned side up.
3 Add butter to the hot frying pan and melt, add king prawns, a little salt and pepper, shake the pan or stir prawns round with a wooden spoon, turn heat up and cook for 2-3 minutes. Add lemon juice by squeezing lemons with hand. If there are pips in the lemons squeeze through a sieve.
4 Take the prawn butter mix off the gas and pour over the turbot. Before serving the fish, place in a hot oven for 4-5 minutes to heat through the fish and prawns.
5 Place fish on a warm plate and divide prawns and butter between portions; sprinkle with chopped chives and serve.

Jim's salt and pepper swordfish

with Asian Greens Steamed in Paper

greaseproof paper
6 swordfish steaks approx 6-8oz
1 bunch spring onions
1 thumb size piece of ginger
2 stalks lemon grass
2 heads pak choi
2 heads bok choi
50 g Chinese cabbage-shredded

light soya sauce
1 tbsp Demerara sugar
20 g unsalted butter
1 tbsp Maldon sea salt
1 tbsp cracked black pepper
1 tbsp crushed Schezuan peppercorns

METHOD

1 Take greaseproof paper and draw 12 circles around 10 or 11" dinner plates and cut out with sharp scissors.
2 Lightly butter each one in the centre, leaving a good 2" gap around the rim.
3 Finely chop ginger and finely slice soft stalk of lemon grass and sweat in butter until starting to turn golden brown, add sugar and soya sauce and simmer for 5 minutes.
4 Fold in chopped whites of spring onions and white parts of bok and pak choi, also fold in Chinese cabbage. Sweat off for further 3 minutes, pour into a metal bowl and cut into 1" pieces adding roughly torn bok and pak choi.
5 Allow to cool and place small handful of mixture into centre of 6 of the paper circles, top with a swordfish steak, sprinkle generously with Maldon salt, cracked pepper and crushed Schezuan peppercorns, top with another small amount of greens, put the other 6 paper circles on top and fold all edges into centre of each circle using approx 1" folds until all edges are secure.
6 Lightly butter top surface of papers and place on buttered metal baking sheet in hot oven for approx 5-7 minutes or until papers have puffed up and are golden brown. Serve straight out of the oven.

Bakewell Tart

SHOPPING LIST

250 g butter
250 g castor sugar
250 g ground almonds
30 g plain flour
60 g raspberry jam
4 medium eggs

METHOD

1 Make pastry case and blind bake.
2 Spread the raspberry jam evenly over the cooked pastry case.
3 Cream the butter and sugar in a mixer until light and fluffy.
4 Crack and whisk the eggs into a small jug and slowly add the egg mixture to the creamed butter and sugar mix.
5 Sieve the flour and fold the ground almonds in gently with a wooden spoon.
6 Spoon the mixture into the jammed pastry case and smooth over.
7 Bake for 1 hour at gas mark 4.
8 Ideally, serve slightly warm with vanilla ice cream or double cream.

Panacotta

40 fl oz double cream
200 g castor sugar
2 vanilla pods
2 leaves gelatin

METHOD

1 Soak the gelatin leaves in cold water.
2 Split and scrape the vanilla pods and place in a thick-bottomed pot with the cream and sugar.
3 Place on gas and bring to the boil, and when boiling remove from heat.
4 Squeeze the gelatin leaves removing any excess water and add the leaves to the hot cream.
5 Pour cream mixture into a jug and stir over a bowl of ice until mixture cools. This helps the vanilla seeds to not sink to the bottom of the cream.
6 When cool, pour into 3½ inch dariole moulds, and chill for 24 hours.
7 To turn out panacotta, let hot water run over sides and base of mould, wet your free fingers and pull panacotta gently from sides of mould and turn out onto plate.
8 Serve with fresh fruit coulis or ideally fresh raspberries with balsamic vinegar.

Raspberry Crème Brulee

360ml double cream
360ml milk
7 egg yolks
105 g granulated sugar
1 vanilla pod (or 1 tsp vanilla essence)
8 raspberries per brulee

METHOD

1 Place egg yolks and sugar in a bowl and whisk together until smooth.
2 Bring milk and cream to boil with split vanilla pod.
3 Pour cream mix onto egg yolks whisking all the time.
4 Put raspberries into ramekins and skim brulee mix making sure there is no froth on top.
5 Pour into ramekins; raspberries may float to the top.
6 Cook in hot oven at gas mark 3/160°C for 35-45 minutes.
7 Before serving sprinkle granulated sugar on top and glaze under a very warm grill, or alternatively use a blowtorch.

Chocolate and Amaretto Mousse

100 g valhrona dark chocolate
100ml amaretto
1 leaf golden gelatine or 2 teaspoons powder
2 cups double cream
1/2 teaspoon ground cinnamon
2 eggs separated
whipped cream
6 amaretto biscuits (optional)

METHOD

1 In a small heat proof bowl combine 100ml amaretto with gelatine and let stand for 5 minutes, then place in a small saucepan of gently simmering water until gelatine dissolves.
2 Gently heat 1 cup of cream with the chocolate in a small saucepan, stirring often until mixture is smooth, then remove from heat and stir in gelatine mixture, cinnamon and egg yolks.
3 Cool mixture to room temperature.
4 Using an electric mixer, whisk remaining cream until soft peaks form, and gently fold into chocolate mixture.
5 Using the clean mixer, whisk egg until soft peaks form, stir one third of whites into chocolate mixture to loosen, then gently fold in remaining egg whites.
6 Divide mixture among six glasses or chocolate pots and refrigerate for 4-6 hours until set.
7 Serve mousse with whipped cream and amaretto biscuit.

Fish stock
(3-4 pints)

SHOPPING LIST

1.8kg fish bones (turbot, lemon sole or monkfish are best)
1 onion, finely chopped
1 leek, finely chopped
1/2 whole bulb of garlic, sliced horizontally

2 litres water
1 lemon, sliced
2 sprigs parsley
1 tbsp. vegetable oil

METHOD

1 Wash the bones very throughly and chop up.
2 Cook the vegetables and garlic in the oil for a few minutes. Do not colour.
3 Add the chopped fish bones and cook without colouring for about five minutes.
4 Add the water and bring to the boil. Skim well, removing any froth.
5 Add the lemon and parsley. Simmer for 20-30 minutes.
6 Pass through a sieve and leave to cool
7 When cool, the stock can be frozen.

Fish Cream
(makes enough for 6)

SHOPPING LIST

1200ml fish stock
300ml white wine
600ml double cream

pinch salt
1 bay leaf

METHOD

1 Bring the fish stock to the boil and reduce to half a pint.
2 Add the white wine and reduce again, by half.
3 Finally add the double cream, simmer and add bay leaf. Reduce to correct pouring consistency.

Meat Stock

1 kilo bones (beef, veal, lamb)
all or any
275g vegetables
(onions, carrots, celery, leeks; all
chopped)
100 g bacon

1 handful parsley
1 tsp. mixed peppercorns
1 tsp. salt
4-5 pints water

METHOD

1 Pre-heat oven to Gas Mark 7, 240°C.
2 Brown the bones and vegetables in a hot oven. Put the bones and bacon rind, vegetables, parsley and peppercorns into a large pan and cover with water.
3 Bring to the boil slowly and simmer for 3-4 hours, skimming all the time to remove froth. Strain and cool. When cold remove any fat.
4 Put into a clean pot and reduce by half. Check seasoning. Freeze left-overs.

Gamba Salad Dressing

SHOPPING LIST

2 cups vegetable or sunflower oil
1 tbsp. sugar
2 tbsp. white wine vinegar
1½ tsp. of English mustard

¼ onion
1 tsp. salt
½ clove garlic

METHOD

1 For this recipe simply blend all ingredients together and pass through a sieve.
2 Keep refrigerated at all times.

List of Recipes

Weights, Measures and Servings

Standards Liquid

1 tsp	=	5ml
1 tbsp	=	15ml
1 fl.oz	=	30ml
1 ml	=	0.35ml
1 pint	=	20 fl.oz
1 litre	=	35 fl.oz

Standards Solid

1 oz	=	30g
1 lb	=	16 oz
1 g	=	0.35 oz
1 kg	=	2.2 lb

Liquid Conversions

Metric	Imperial
15ml	$\frac{1}{2}$ fl.oz
30ml	1 fl.oz
50ml	$1\,\frac{2}{3}$ fl.oz
100ml	$3\,\frac{1}{3}$ fl.oz
250ml	8 fl.oz
500ml	$16\,\frac{2}{3}$ fl.oz
600ml	20 fl.oz (1 pint)
1 litre	$1\,\frac{3}{4}$ pints

Solid Weight Conversions

Metric	Imperial
5g	$\frac{1}{6}$ oz
10g	$\frac{1}{3}$ oz
15g	$\frac{1}{2}$ oz
30g	1 oz
50g	$1\,\frac{2}{3}$ oz
60g	2 oz
90g	3 oz
100g	$3\,\frac{1}{3}$ oz
250g	$8\,\frac{1}{3}$ oz
500g	$16\,\frac{2}{3}$ oz

Oven Temperature Conversions

°C	Gas	°F
110	$\frac{1}{4}$	225
120	$\frac{1}{2}$	250
140	1	275
150	2	300
160	3	325
175	4	350
190	5	375
200	6	400
220	7	425
230	8	450
240	9	475
260	10	500

All weights, measures and servings are approximate conversions